OSTRICH

Sandie Lee Books

Ostriches

They may look like something out of a weird story, but the ostrich is a real bird. This bird is classed as a ratite. They are closely related to the rhea, emu, cassowary and the kiwi birds. Ostriches were once thought to bury their heads in the sand to hide, but this isn't so. The ostrich needs to bend low to the ground to feed, so this caused an optical illusion of its head being hidden. Let's explore some more cool facts about this unusual bird.

Where in the World?

Did you know ostriches live in Africa? These mighty birds like dry sandy terrain. In Africa, they will wander the savannas and desert regions. This species of bird can often be found with herds of wildebeest, antelopes and zebras. These animals dig up insects while they are grazing (which the ostrich eats) and the ostrich alerts them to predators.

The Body of an Ostrich

Did you know the ostrich is the biggest bird in the world? It stands a whopping 9 feet tall and it can weigh as much as 350 pounds. It has a very long neck and legs. The short wings of the ostrich cannot make it fly, but they do balance it when it runs.

Ostrich Eyes

Did you know the eyes of an ostrich are bigger than its brain? The ostrich has the biggest eyes of all the land mammals. Its eyes are about as big as a billiard ball. These leave very little room in its small head for its brain. However, since it is so tall, it can see predators from a great distance away.

What an Ostrich Eats

Did you know the ostrich eats pebbles to help digest its food? Small pebbles go into the gizzard of the ostrich - this is a special place in its stomach. The small stones help break down the food so it can be easily digested. Ostriches also eat seeds, insects, small lizards, grass, fruit and some flowers.

The Ostrich's Special Ability

Did you know one of the ostrich's running strides equals 16 feet! What the ostrich lacks in flight skills it makes up for with its speed. An ostrich can run over 40 miles-per-hour in short sprints and 30 miles-per-hour over a great distance. The wings of the ostrich not only help it balance, but they provide insulation from the heat.

Ostrich Power

Did you know ostriches have special feet? Unlike most birds that have 3 or 4 toes on each foot, the ostrich only has 2 toes on each foot. Each one of these toes also has a long sharp claw. This is used for defense against predators. Ostriches can give a powerful kick that can even kill a lion.

The Ostrich as Prey

Did you know the ostrich is hunted? Even though the ostrich is a huge bird, animals like lions, cheetahs, crocodiles and hyenas will hunt them. Although, it is a difficult task, younger and older ostriches can be taken by wild predators. Humans also hunt the ostrich for its meat and feathers.

Ostrich Talk

Did you know ostriches can make sounds? They have been known to whistle, snort and hiss, plus they can make a booming sound. This is done by the male in mating season. He will inflate his neck to three times its normal size, then boom his voice out. This can be heard for great distances.

Ostrich Mom

Did you know the mother ostrich is called a hen? Female ostriches lay their eggs in a communal nest. The dominate female lays her eggs in the middle of the nest - this is to ensure they have the best chance of hatching. One female ostrich will sit on the nest, while the male stands guard.

Ostrich Eggs

Did you know one ostrich egg is as big as 24 chicken eggs? Ostrich eggs measure about 6 inches long and 5 inches wide. Each one weighs about 3 pounds and are the biggest eggs in the world. They are very white and shiny. This keeps them from overheating when exposed to the sun.

Ostrich Baby

Did you know ostrich babies hatch already knowing how to walk? The chicks are covered with feathers and leave the nest within days of hatching. The chicks follow the adult ostriches around and learn how to hunt for food. When it is rainy or hot, the chicks huddle under their mother's wings.

Ostrich at Rest

Did you know ostriches can sleep with their eyes open? Studies have shown that even though an ostrich may appear to be awake, it can actually be sleeping. When an ostrich goes into a deep sleep, its neck will droop and its eyes will close. Ostriches also like to rest with their necks stretched out on the ground.

Life of an Ostrich

Did you know ostriches gather in flocks? These flocks can be from 10 up to 100 members. In these flocks, there will be a dominate male and a dominant female. The ostrich also has a long lifespan. It can live from 20 to 40 years in the wild. In captivity, some ostrich have lived for over 50 years of age.

Red-necked Ostrich

This type of ostrich is the largest subspecies of all the ratite. This ostrich is also called the North African ostrich. They can be found from the east to the west of Africa. The female's plumage is grey in color. Both the males and the females of this bird have red skin on their necks.

Quiz

Question 1: Where in the world does the ostrich live?

Answer 1: In Africa on sandy terrain - deserts and savannas

Question 2: The ostrich is the largest bird in the world. How big can it get?

Answer 2: It can be 9 feet tall and weigh up to 350 pounds

Question 3: How big are the ostrich's eyes?

Answer 3: Its eyes are as big as a billiard ball

Question 4: What is special about the ostrich's feet?

Answer 4: It has 2 twos on each foot

Question 5: Why does the male ostrich make a booming sound?

Answer 5: To attract a mate

Thank you for checking out another addition from Sandie Lee Books! Make sure to check out Amazon.com for many other great titles.